E

AUSTRALIAN

A POCKET GUIDE TO TRANSLATING ENGLISH TO ENGLISH

So you don't look stupid
when trying to understand
British English words

PREFACE

Most Britons travelling to Australia don't expect there to be a language barrier but there are more differences in British vs Australian words than you think. This mini illustrated 'dictionary' is here to rescue you.

CHEERS!

ABSOLUTELY

RECKON

ACCIDENT

PRANG

AFTERNOON

ARVO

ALCOHOL

GROG

AMERICAN

YANK

ANGRY

BERKO

AUSTRALIA

STRALIA

AUSTRALIAN

AUSSIE

AUSTRALIAN MAN

BRUCE

AVOCADO

AVO

BANANA

NANA

BARBEQUE

BARBIE

BED LINEN

MANCHESTER

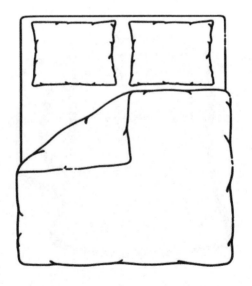

BEER

AMBER

BEER

A COLD ONE

BEER GLASS

POT

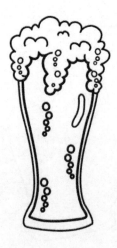

BISCUIT

BIKKIE

BREAD

DAMPER

BRILLIANT

BONZA

BROKEN

CACTUS

CATTLE FARM TRAINEE
TRAINEE

JACKAROO

CHEAP WINE

PLONK

CHILD

ANKLE BITER

CRIMINAL

BUSHRANGER

CHICKEN

CHOOK

CHOCOLATE

CHOKKIE

CHRISTMAS

CHRISSIE

CIGARETTE BREAK

SMOKO

COMPLAIN

GRIZZLE

CAR ENGINE

DONK

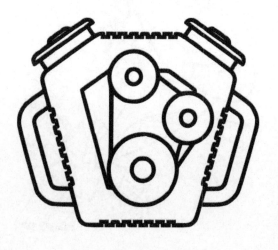

ENGLISH
PERSON

POM

EUCALYPTUS TREE

GUM TREE

EXACT INFORMATION

GOOD OIL

FARM

STATION

FLIP FLOPS

THONGS

FOOD

TUCKER

FOREST

BUSH

GARAGE

SERVO

GIVE UP

GIVE AWAY

GO AWAY

RACK OFF

GO AWAY

SHOVE OFF

GOOD JOB

GOOD LURK

GREAT

YOU BEAUTY!

HAVE A LOOK

GANDER

HELLO

G'DAY MATE

HIKING

BUSHWALKING

HOOLIGAN

HOON

HORSES

NEDDIES

HOW ARE YOU?

HOW ARE YOU GOING?

IDIOT

DRONGO

INFORMATION

OIL

KANGAROO

ROO

KETTLE

BILLIE

KISS

PASH

LONG TIME

YONKS

MANY

HEAPS

MCDONALDS

MACCAS

MIDDLE OF NOWHERE

BACK OF BOURKE

MILKMAN

MILKO

MONEY

LOLLY

MOSQUITO

MOZZIE

NAKED

NUDDY

NEW ZEALANDER

KIWI

NONSENSE

PIFFLE

NO WORRIES

NO WUCKAS

OFF-LICENCE

BOTTLE O

OFF-LICENCE

BOTTLE SHOP

OK

RIGHTIO

PANTS (MEN)

JOCKS

PEE

SNAKES HISS

POSTMAN

POSTIE

PUB MEAL

COUNTER MEAL

RELATIVES

RELLIES

RUBBISH COLLECTOR

GARBO

SANDWICHES

CUT LUNCH

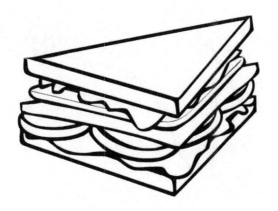

SAUSAGE

SNAG

SHARK MEAT

FLAKE

SHEEP DOG

KELPIE

SHEEP
FARMER

WOOL GROWER

SHUT UP

BELT UP

SNAKE

JOE BLAKE

SOLDIER

DIGGER

STUPID
PERSON

ALF

SUNGLASSES

SUNNIES

SUV

UTE

SWEETS

LOLLIES

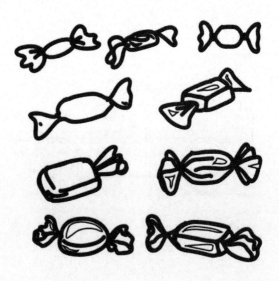

SWIMMING COSTUME

BATHERS

TEACHER

CHALKIE

TIRED

ROOTED

TOILET

COMFORT STATION

TOILET

DUNNY

TRAINERS

RUNNERS

TROUSERS

DAKS / STRIDES

TRUE

DEADSET

UNDERTAKER

MORTICIAN

U-TURN

U-IE

VEGETABLES

VEGGIES

VERY HAPPY

RAPT

WELL DONE

GOOD ON YA

WOMAN

SHEILA

WORN OUT

ROOTED

Printed in Great Britain
by Amazon